** Special black page to avoid bleed-through **

THIS BOOK BELONGS TO

Creative Design Press

** Special black page to avoid bleed-through **

** Special black page to avoid bleed-through **

** Special black page to avoid bleed-through **

** Special black page to avoid bleed-through **

** Special black page to avoid bleed-through **

** Special black page to avoid bleed-through **

** Special black page to avoid bleed-through **

** Special black page to avoid bleed-through **

** Special black page to avoid bleed-through **

** Special black page to avoid bleed-through **

** Special black page to avoid bleed-through **

** Special black page to avoid bleed-through **

** Special black page to avoid bleed-through **

** Special black page to avoid bleed-through **

** Special black page to avoid bleed-through **

** Special black page to avoid bleed-through **

** Special black page to avoid bleed-through **

** Special black page to avoid bleed-through **

** Special black page to avoid bleed-through **

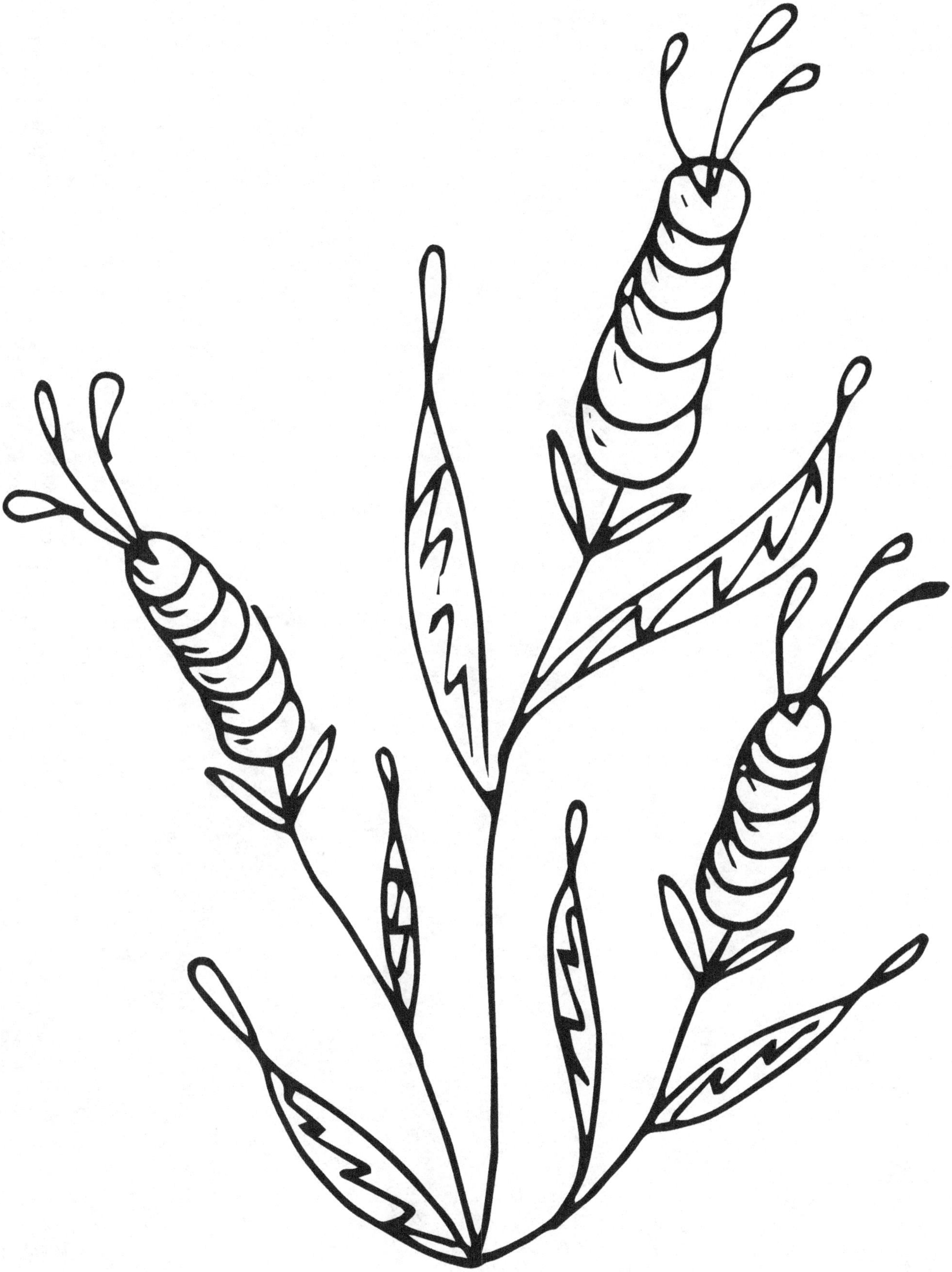

** Special black page to avoid bleed-through **

** Special black page to avoid bleed-through **

** Special black page to avoid bleed-through **

** Special black page to avoid bleed-through **

** Special black page to avoid bleed-through **

** Special black page to avoid bleed-through **

** Special black page to avoid bleed-through **

Made in the USA
Monee, IL
26 September 2022

14686594R00037